IN THE REALM OF NEITHER

other books by the author

Poetry:
Dawn Visions
Burnt Heart/Ode to the War Dead
This Body of Black Light Gone Through the Diamond
The Desert is the Only Way Out
The Chronicles of Akhira
Halley's Comet
Awake as Never Before
The Ramadan Sonnets
The Blind Beekeeper
Mars & Beyond
Laughing Buddha Weeping Sufi
Salt Prayers
Ramadan Sonnets (The Ecstatic Exchange revised edition)
Psalms for the Brokenhearted
I Imagine a Lion
Coattails of the Saint
Abdallah Jones and the Disappearing-Dust Caper
Love is a Letter Burning in a High Wind
The Flame of Transformation Turns to Light
Underwater Galaxies
The Music Space
Cooked Oranges
Through Rose Colored Glasses
Like When You Wave at a Train and the Train Hoots Back at You
In the Realm of Neither

Theater / The Floating Lotus Magic Opera Company:
The Walls Are Running Blood
Bliss Apocalypse

Puppet Theater:
The Mystical Romance of Layla & Majnun
The Journey to Qalbiyya

Compilation of Quotes: Warrior Wisdom
Prose: Zen Rock Gardening
The Little Book of Zen
Zen Wisdom

IN THE REALM
OF NEITHER

poems

May 14 – November 12, 2006

Daniel Abdal-Hayy Moore

The Ecstatic Exchange
2008
Philadelphia

In The Realm of Neither
Copyright © 2008 Daniel Abdal-Hayy Moore
All rights reserved.
Printed in the United States of America

For quotes any longer than those for critical articles and reviews, contact:
The Ecstatic Exchange,
6470 Morris Park Road, Philadelphia, PA 19151-2403
email: abdalhayy@danielmoorepoetry.com

First Edition
ISBN: 978-0-6152-2182-3 (paper)
Published by *The Ecstatic Exchange*,
6470 Morris Park Road, Philadelphia, PA 19151-2403

Acknowledgements:
An Antelope Grew Tired of Loping first appeared in Mizna, Vol. 8, Issue 2, 2006, and the poems *Great Cruelty and Heartlessness, The Enormous Corridor of Sorrow, Birds Burst into Flower, Love Excruciating As It Is* and *World Split Apart* appeared in prose poem form in Islamica Magazine, Issue 18, 2006. *Noah's Music* appeared in Seasons Journal, Spring 2008.

Also available from The Ecstatic Exchange:
Knocking from Inside, poems by Tiel Aisha Ansari

Cover and text design by Abdallateef Whiteman / www.ianwhiteman.com
Cover collage by the author
Back cover photo by Omar Mullick

DEDICATION

To
Shaykh ibn al-Habib
(and the continuation of the Habibiyya)
Shaykh Bawa Muhaiyuddeen,
all shuyukh of instruction and ma'arifa
and
Baji Tayyaba Khanum
and the eternal lineage

❖

*The earth is not bereft
of Light*

CONTENTS

Author's Note on the Title   10

1	Last Train	13
2	Let Me Curl up Around Death	15
3	The Roar of Engines	16
4	God's Alchemy	18
5	Fantastic Urn	19
6	Why the Sun Only Shines in Certain Places	20
7	The Long Smooth Board	22
8	Becoming the Mountain	27
9	Everyone's Given Their Own Set of Eyes	33
10	The Eye Sees	36
11	The Name of the Rose	37
12	Piracy Brigandage and Banditry	39
13	How Many Angels	41
14	Zurich Bird	44
15	Out the Airplane Window	45
16	Ten Short Reality Checks	52
17	Noah's Music	55
18	But We Know Better	58
19	Monumental Day	60
20	The Late Middle and Early People	62
21	Hail the Explorers	67
22	Perspective	70

23	Problems of Translation	71
24	Singular Shadow	73
25	Sphinx Thoughts	75
26	Great Cruelty and Heartlessness	76
27	What Bugs Will Eat Me	78
28	Angelic Physics	79
29	The Enormous Corridor of Sorrow	81
30	Polar Opposites	83
31	Birds Burst into Flower	84
32	Love Excruciating As It Is	86
33	World Split Apart	88
34	An Antelope Grew Tired of Loping	91
35	Bug Gratitude	93
36	Flower of Languages	94
37	Serpent in the Plumbing	96
38	The Elves Have Taken the Earth Away	98
39	The Arrow	100
40	He Races to the Edge	101
41	Seismograph	103
42	Death's Door	105
43	I Sang	106
44	The Lighthouse Widow's Pronouncements	108
45	The Turning	110
46	Looking and Seeing	113
47	Camping Trip	115
48	Dot	116
49	Seed	118

50	What Then?	119
51	The Island	122
52	The Cat's Gone Mad	124
53	And of the Little That We Do	126
54	Riddled With Bullets	129
55	I Should Be Asleep	130
56	Song of Departures	132
57	Shadow Man	134
58	Bone	136
59	Pillars of Cloud	137
60	Fragile Scattering Beads	138
61	Starting With Seven Elegant Cows	140
62	At the House of the Lord	144
63	The Heart Knows	146
64	The Creator's Glittering Hieroglyph	147
65	Flakes	149
66	Time's Wheel	150
67	Written in the Dark at the Fez Music Concert	152
68	Ultra Short Edda	154
69	Beard	157
70	Perfect Tiny Blue Rose	158
71	In the Air and on Earth	162
72	Job Waited by the Door	164
73	What the Table Holds	167
74	When There's Nothing to Say	169
75	The Shape of the Rose Garden	171

76	A Spark in Your Being	173
77	Two	174
78	Don't Forget Chumley	175
79	If All the Wood in the World	178
80	Swimming On	181
81	Impossible to Sleep	183
82	Kind of Person	186
83	Held in Thrall	188
84	Waking	191
85	In the Realm of Neither	192

AUTHOR'S NOTE ON THE TITLE

I HAD A DREAM just before waking of a shelf filled with books, and I was reading the titles when a spotlight hit the spine of one book that also seemed to protrude from the others and be coming out of the shelf toward me. On it were the words *"In the Realm of Neither"* that remained vivid and unforgettable upon waking.

For some reason the title resonates, and reminds me of a very weighty study by Michael A. Sells, *Mystical Languages of Unsaying*, in which the Divine Creator/Principle/Entity is best defined by an eloquently theological refusal to name it (an *apophatic* "saying away"), focusing instead on *not* saying rather than saying, and by that negative space spotlighting and somehow delineating the ineffable divine positive. It also evokes the *Not This Not That* of early Hindu wise recognitions as well as the Taoist admonition against naming the Tao, *That Which Can't Be Named*.

My own Islamic Sufi path is one in which the generosity has been given us by Allah to call on Him by His Name, and even Ninety-Nine Names, Whose reality and essence is still beyond human naming, and for Whom the definition by great and saintly scholars has often been at the highest intensity of enigma, but Who has Named Himself through the Prophet Muhammad, peace and blessings of Allah be upon him, for the rectification and mercifully intimate solace of humankind, while yet retaining that indefinably awesome quality.

Yet at the same time, the title is a conundrum: *Neither what?* Neither night nor day, life or death, God or no God? Does it then point to a space beyond the dichotomies, the place of pure Unity, which transcends by incorporating and embracing all opposites? The alive sacred space before all theologies kick in, and when they have reached their enlightened goal of the space before theologies kick in, which is purity and really ineffable, ecstatic and singular? The Sufis say "There is nothing *but* Allah, no other *than* Allah," and yet the manifest world is *not* Allah, but just that, His manifestation, all the Names of God in activated process and epiphany. So this "neither" is not God, but neither is it *not* God. And so on. Bringing us always back to our own hearts and our own created selves. And as the Prophet Muhammad said, peace be upon him, "*He who knows himself, knows his Lord…*" that has innumerable ramifications which our lives play out in multifarious ways.

Now, I'm not sure that the poems in this collection live up to the title, but because of its evocative nature, from whose energy the writing of the poems has been somehow propelled, I've kept it and let its enticing and evocative "conundrumous" nature stand.

Some of these poems were written during the tragically over-reacted invasion of Lebanon by the Israeli army, and were read publicly in solidarity with the Lebanese people: *Great Cruelty and Heartlessness, The Enormous Corridor of Sorrow, Birds Burst into Flower, Love Excruciating As It Is, World Split Apart* and *An Antelope Grew Tired of Loping*.

I pray that God allow us to work to His sweet satisfaction, and as Van Gogh prayed regarding *his* art, and I concur, that these poems be useful.

May 24, 2008

When you define God, you negate Him, because you make Him equal to things that have been defined.
— ADONIS, SUFISM AND SURREALISM

Verily, He causes the sustenance to descend upon me, and I see Him flowing through the whale in the water and through the bird in the sky.
— SHAYKH ABU AL-HASAN AL-SHADHILI

1 LAST TRAIN

Having set out constitutes only half the solution

The next half comes in vivid increments as the
window images flash by each with a

secret memorandum attached though not
obvious to the onlooker

But getting on the train and in a forward direction
and seeing the world pull away
is no small matter

The tallest waterfall in the world just flashed by
its peak covered in perpetual mist

The most golden late-autumn landscape imaginable
and the whitest most ubiquitously glittering meadow

and the most desolate heat-drenched arroyo and the
most populated minefield metropolis

have all come to nothing

Yet this isn't the death train and
makes no stops for death

It's the last train to Seattle
but you won't take it

It's the last train to the starriest
source of night but no passengers get on or off

There's one more seat left
and each seat must be occupied

Great wings surround it
in loving embrace

At the end of the tunnel is a light

And at the end of the light
a tunnel

5/14

2 LET ME CURL UP AROUND DEATH

Let me curl up around death
and make peace with it

All the wonderful things I'll have to leave
when I die

The purring of our cat
my wife's breath

The sense of patterns in the air

Their balustrades of sensible sweetness
and occasional gardens

out of pure space

Their forward motion

                              5/16

3 THE ROAR OF ENGINES

"The roar of engines shall not
drown out my ardor" said the lover to
his beloved both fleshy and metaphysical

"The falling of towers both down and up
shall not shake my equilibrium" said the
serene student of esoterica and plain fact

"One door open and one door closed
shall not deter my resolve to reach the
goal" shouted in complete silence
the devotee facing a wall with only the
hint of a smile

"Uphill and downhill are the same to a
gust of wind though shutters shake and
umbrellas break" sang slightly off key
the mystical meteorologist standing by her
weather map in the darkened studio

"Nowhere is where to He Who is everywhere"
mentioned in passing the old forgotten
stranger walking slowly off to the left

with his withered hand on his
gnarled cane

into pale green sunlight

                                              5/18

4 GOD'S ALCHEMY

Green elements turn into golden ones when
God's breath flows across them

Gold dust motes float down as slowly as
elephants sinking into mud for a cooling bath

The whole golden earth turns its face to the dark
as its spine stands still and its tilt wobbles slightly

We turn our faces to the sunlight once or twice in a
day if our hearts are slow in jumping over turnstiles

I look up at the Spring trees and see some
leaves where the sun shines through turn

transparently golden

O God shine through us the way
the sun shines through these transparent leaves and

ignites them
and turns them golden

5/22

5 FANTASTIC URN

You can see the fantastic urn
out in the meadow
that was used to carry the ashes

The caparisoned horse team and silver wagon
as the mist curls around them

On descending bleachers the living and
dead who've come to honor him
and the clear white sky glaring above him

And the city beyond them shimmering in
smoke and sunlight

And the procession of people with heads bowed
who've come to honor him

5/26

6 WHY THE SUN ONLY SHINES IN CERTAIN PLACES

Not due to rotundity nor morbidity certainly
nor the fact that we walk upright through
door or corridor picking our
teeth as we go or solving difficult theorems
though to tell the truth the sunlight *does*

tend to favor the *aha!* moment over
humdrum factual stasis

A crisp wasp wrapped itself around a tasty morsel
on a sunlit leaf and saw thereby its
momentary quota of God's provision edibly manifest
and gave adequate thanks before
speeding away thus tipping the animate
universe that one thankful expansion more
in favor of general gratitude which

makes the seven seas flow backwards and forwards on
time and clocks strike eleven at precisely eleven and not
twelve or ten or another moot number

and dolphins arch themselves before
diving and show a glistening spine to the
sunlight in full splendor

and at a window a young scholar sees the
pages of his book illumined and so
also his heart with radiant calm

This simplified memorandum to set ourselves
out where the sun does shine rather than
where it doesn't and to

let that light that does leak into less
accessible places also

radiate calm

            5/29

7   THE LONG SMOOTH BOARD

I

The long smooth board that connects the worlds
no not a smooth board but rugged

mountain peaks where some parties have been
lost for ages gazing eagleward when

earthward and homeward would have better served

The gorges and hyper-altitudes dark lanes and
crooked byways and even the still small cells

where one anchorite sits in deepest contemplation
as ants deconstruct his house and

reconstruct it again on the underside of a leaf

The sunlight lodge in between this world and the
next where generators of living activity keep the

buzz on or the sudden oceans between bathers
or the sudden swarming continents between oceans

even the rarely blinking reptilian survivors on the
Galapagos Islands basking forever on iron-black rocks

All these uncanny connections and connectors between
worlds presided over by a wise snail in

snail regalia who very slowly leads us from
one step to another until we're

bathed in the supersensory exaltation of the
bliss of both worlds and can see with our

own eyes the absolute glory at the farthest
end of each

2

So what are these worlds if not the
usual dichotomy the usual

this-world next-world light-world dark-world
life and death tango where sometimes

death steps too far forward and bends life
too far back leaving decimated dancers who had

so much hope when the sad music started

But we see it as if on a bare stage with
one spotlight and all the supporting players now

coming out of shadows then turning and
going back into them again forever

Or the way a song comes and animates our
innermost vocal chords accompanied by a

tingling heartbeat and it seems even the
clouds are clapping vaporous hands in time to our music

Then thunder and darkness hit and
some of us stand still
and some of us keep moving forward unfazed

Still the point of contact between them is neither
one nor the other

a shaft filled with swallows in vertical flight

the sibilant hiss of a water heater at
night in the Swiss kitchen where I

write this without a thought in my head
but a faith somehow that enough water will

flush across the rocks to
make a fully roaring cascade

3

Even the wombat baby in the bush knows this
and the Himalayan heron chased by two

golden eagles in a sunlit updraft to its
final overpowering by both knows this

Each breath taken in knows this as it
relinquishes its hold after its generalized aeration

and lets it out again into the awaiting universe
carbon dioxide rich and sitting among its

jewels like a thief in silks

The two worlds intermingle in an offhand
moment in the crash of oil cruet on a

glass restaurant table

In the opera singer in
the middle of her aria who suddenly

isn't there in any experiential way
only the song is
breathing so naturally out of her

that the entire audience
feels it in its bones

and is
no longer afraid

                                                                6/3

8 BECOMING THE MOUNTAIN

I

Everyone knew the altitude and topography
the very scale of the thing was so far
beyond him yet he continued to
aspire to become the mountain

they saw each day from their windows first
thing after dawn and last thing before
sunset and some grazed their sheep at its
base in rolling valleys and narrow
gorges and repeatedly suggested to him that
these mild levels would be enough but

he wasn't satisfied

It had no name he could formulate his grand
desire from early childhood to not just
climb it but be it take it on bodily

A mountain generally snow-capped and
mist-covered whose top formations of
peak and rocky scowl frightened many
alpinists and lesser adventurers and

behind whose brooding silhouette often dazzled
gigantic rays of really an otherworldly

light a spiky halo of incandescence that
reached into every household and
took hold of every heart

2

Only angels could possibly know it as it
should be known

its icy flanks and sheer drops and jutting
crags and its easy lounging across such
horizontal distances as if in a bituminous caravan

stretching from sunrise to sunset

Yet in his modest ways he changed his
stature and by vigilance reduced his
actual height which in itself could
never hope to approximate the mountain

seeing through his eyes more exalted vistas
his mind's thoughts not turning in the usual endless

rotations over known territories of
memory and resentment but actually
cutting ropes and tossing ballast enough to
begin not just the perilous climb but
also the inner approximation

to the way clouds gather and disperse
and the way sunlight cuts in gleaming

swords directly down through the serrated edges of rock
into the valleys below

3

Never underestimate the power of
impossible desire

Flight would never have occurred to us nor
loss of lesser self with God's encompassing

Presence and ultimate All-pervasiveness
in every domain of our being

Saying what was unknown to us before
on prophetic tongues out of our usual human shallows

turning the tragic momentariness of our life
into a cup of delicious and deliriously

tasted expansion the wine of His illumination and
the drink that slakes all thirsts in a

single swallow by His Grace
the heart's tongue becoming suddenly capable of

choirs

4

Sometimes the peak is shrouded in mist
the sheer size overpowering

Even airplanes sometimes miss the free air channel
over it and collide with its cliffs

There are birds that exist nowhere else
but at its heights in wheeling ever-presence

It can't be exactly pinpointed on any map

And everyone's ascent is particular to
his or her spirit and the circumstances of
his or her climb from birth

Some may not even want to climb and find the prospect
barely worthy of their attention

The old texts speak of it as *The Cloud of Unknowing*
The Tao That Cannot Be Called A Name
Neither This Nor That

And even the Name we've been given to
Call on Allah has clouds around it on a

clear day

Though it be a sound so pure it pierces vapor
and rolls off the tongue more sweetly than
any known combination of flavors or even

any total absence of flavor
He being said to be *The Pronoun of Absence*
so as not to confound it with a created person
though it be even for Him a

Personal Pronoun

as fire-sparks illuminate rotating red
circles in the black of night and deep

purple pinwheels turn in a sea depth of deep velvet
darkness and a golden fish of clarity in a
stretch of obscurity so soot black as to be
a total blindness stands still in its own light

He is neither *This nor That* and yet He is *All
and None*

And with that the child at the top of his
globe of the world starts moving forward

counterclockwise to the purpose of his life on earth
in order to achieve it

and zebras run across open plains
white stripes against black or black stripes against white

we'll never know for sure
though the spectacle be elementally enthralling

and the dust rising from their stampeding hooves
in its light airy earthiness like the

mist at the mountain peak he has become at last
connect in their atoms to the

simple answer of his heart's irresolvable conundrum

6/6

9 EVERYONE'S GIVEN THEIR OWN SET OF EYES

Everyone's given their own set of eyes
to see through

from the lake of the heart its mercury mirror
aslant slightly to tilt back God's Light

which is what we see by that small
special glitter in the eyes visible to

other eyes and their actual illumination
by which we see the gliding black

red-beaked bird that lives in the
high Alps as it wheels in gray sky

looking for scraps or tourist handouts

and then over enormous distances in one
glance and that glance may not be

even physical nor this seeing at all be
completely physical as when the

Prophet saw the seventy thousand
veils of light and darkness at the

Ascension and saw out over Jerusalem and
remembered its layout later to prove his

supernatural visit there may Allah be pleased with him a
thousand times over

These little eyes of ours also like treasures not
enumerated in Ali Baba's cave among the

rubies and topazes tumbling from its chests
these eyes of ours more precious by far than any jewel

seeing red flamingos on a green hillside with their
heads tucked underneath their wings

or glittering glints of light like a billion
flakes of other worlds on the surface of a

rushing cascade from a nearby mountain height
all things visual and all things supervisual

The shaft of illumination that makes itself into a
walkable stairway over this abysmal world

into charted particles of auditory splendor
ambiently scattering the clear voice of One God

all around us in myriad movements

each glimpse of glamorous planetary motion
or nebula splattered in space its golden or

scarlet nimbus in blackness

each sight of a beloved's uplit face catching
sight of us seeing their two eyes

happily seeing back at us in the same moment
in time and space

6/7

10 THE EYE SEES

The eye sees what Allah sees

The mouth speaks the self's mortal interference

6/7

11 THE NAME OF THE ROSE

*"The name of the rose on her lips as she
sank into darkness was…"*

but the dream phrase left upon waking
was cut off before the crucial word was

heard and only the teaser remembered
so that I wonder at times at human

knowledge also that we're often left with
just the teaser that is so pregnant with

meaning but whose pith is somehow obscured
and like flags waving in a breeze

we're left with the commotion but without the
import that will give all humankind such

ease we're left with the motion in the air such
phrases make such cogitations but without

swimming up into them to finish the
sentence with our bodies as it were and thus embody the

very name of the rose whatever it might be
"*courage*" came to mind when I awoke but it

wasn't "*courage*" so that it might also be
"*intuition*" or "*pure volition*" or even a symbolically

charged name like "*The name of the rose is
white light in a dark place*" or

"*The black petaled stallion of forbearance*"
"*The magnificent lion's mane of compassionate radiance*"

or just "*The name of the rose is The Name*"
and let that stand in space as is with all its

attendant but obscure reverberations

we can't know for sure until the rose scent
overwhelm us and

we swoon into the original rosy
alphabetization of our being

6/7

12 PIRACY BRIGANDAGE AND BANDITRY

On the roadways Moldavian bandits
wear the disguise of noblewomen in
hoop skirts of giant yards of taffeta and
swoop down on our carriages singing
popular arias and swinging feathery fans

On the high seas Malaysian pirates
dress as dolphins with that benevolent
smile of theirs and those
neutral eyes and happy noses leaping in
front of the prows of our ships in
intricate dolphin calculation of such things as
sprays and wakes which they
dive through with ease

In the remote Sahara palm trees solemnly
waving their fronds around the sloshing
placid oasis may be brigands unless they're
over eight feet tall in which case they
might simply be trees minding their own silently
barking motherly business after all

So in this world of various forms of
piracy brigandage and banditry

one must have keen eyes and a
watchful tongue to tell truth from lies and thus
unravel life's various subterfuges from which we

walk away fleeced of all our superficial riches
almost down to bare skin in our

own disguises as neutral participants when in fact
we're actually in deep cahoots with the most

radical deceivers in regards to taking
illusion as real in the textural scheme of

things and in both the ultimate meaning and the
ultimate outcome of all this

elegant and inelegant display our own
banditry often hidden from us though the

dust be rising all around us of the
hooves of onslaught horses out of dark woods with

the bandit Truth's muskets already
drawn against us

6/9

13 HOW MANY ANGELS

It's not so much how many angels can dance on the
head of a pin but rather

how many angels on silver bicycles on top of
incandescent balls revolving at terrific

velocities while letting banners stream out behind them
with every event that's about to take

place listed both chronologically and
alphabetically simultaneously

and who's involved and how they
got involved in the first place and

how and where each story ends and how and where it's
picked up again in a cycle that

rotates as fast as they bicycle
Wheels in whose spokes clattering cunningly are not

playing cards nor even Tarot cards stuck between
them to make that truly nostalgic and

haunting sound of our human childhood careening down
hills with *"Look no hands!"* on handle bars and

no feet on the pedals only those angels aren't
even actually sitting on the seats and

yet it all goes smoothly and the
astronomical number of them on the

heads of pins is actually greater for each
one than the number of heads of pins might

exist at any one time on our beloved planet
spinning here in space like the sparkle on a

head of a pin out among the zillion or so
galaxies and stars each no more or

less numerous than these hyperactive
angels are so acrobatically splendid in their

Cirque du Ciel circling ministrations
carrying out the will of their Lord

with the sung out playing-card fluttering
wing sound in space of

God's Names each recited incessantly between their
bicycle spokes heard or unheard by

us on each pin we might hold for a
moment between forefinger and thumb

as we prick our thumbs inadvertently
and a perfect liquid ruby catches

the reflection for a fleeting moment of the
entire universe on its red surface before

turning to radiant light

6/12

14 ZURICH BIRD

That single bird out there
in the Zurich dawn

is very carefully going over
the rules of flight

and where you can land

In Italy the birds
chatter about everything

just as surprised themselves
at their

outbursts of melodious
song

6/13
(Zurich, Switzerland)

15 OUT THE AIRPLANE WINDOW

1

Out the airplane window are white clouds
as if we'd entered an all-white world

but we can't be sure since inside a plane you
only see a few squares of sky at a time

and the linebacker type in the seat in
front of me is pressing back on his seat

so hard it's leaning practically into my lap
and the sound all around us is as if we were

inside a huge ocean wave with possibly some
surfers on top riding its gigantic unrolling conch shell of

water into a sandy shore

and I'm thinking of a story of a man who
lived in a hole and couldn't see either

earth or sky except what he saw at eye-level
though to him it was the entire world

and no one could convince him otherwise
and that's the way it would always

be for him though there were evident
signs to the contrary such as sun and

moon whose thin light to him filtered into his
hole in their diurnal and nocturnal cycles

which he simply took for granted and faint splotches of
stars also seeming to him were decorative touches in an

otherwise unrelieved blackness of the night sky
he saw squinting up above his vacuous domicile

Things placed themselves around him at his
disposal such as chair and bed and table as well as

some mismatched silverware and he felt they owed it to him to
present themselves in service to him so

it didn't occur to him that he
slept and had dreams that might suggest a

realm either behind or beyond the realm he
took as his only home

It didn't occur to him that all these walls and
doors were really passages or obstructions between

worlds or that coming from an origin he was also
traveling toward a place past his final

worldly destination

Just as we are on this airplane from
Zurich to Philadelphia via London Heathrow on a

Tuesday in June having come from somewhere
before and going to somewhere where

Philadelphia doesn't figure at all though it be
a pleasant place for a sojourn and we

live there in a house we call our own
as contented as snow falling onto snow or

water finding its level and lying in a pool

2

Various people came you know
representatives of this or that idea

to jog him from his torpor or unhinge the
scales from his eyes as it were

to see past or through or even into
That Which Is to get even a

rough idea of what it is to be *in* the
world but not *of* it

and so rise out of the hole he's in like
Yusuf in the well as Rumi says

when all of Egypt lies out there waiting for him
to arrive and be its Just Magistrate

But our man's fixed ideas about self and
non-self and even a sliver of an

idea about God that was more of a

fragmented reflection of himself in less perhaps
photorealistic detail thus promoting a

more cloudy conception which he could
maintain in a vaguer mental terrain

All these fixed ideas were tightly screwed
into the walls of his hole like a

fake movie set in which he might
act out his life but not activate

an almost indefinable but essential
element which soon overcomes all others

and could be called perhaps
"slant openings that allow God-rays through"

transforming his perceptual hole into a humble
palace of associations that all lead

back to really what amounts in the end as in
the beginning

to pure glory

3

The hole remains a hole resolutely a hole
year after year a hole

and nothing but a hole

however much we wish it wouldn't
however much we want to invert it for him and
make it more of a skylight overhead or an
overturned kiddy pool at least he could still see
light shining through even if pink or chartreuse

But this *Deep-Down One* this *Hole-Dweller* has not only
made it his home but also if he should

happen to miraculously roam free of it at some point he would
walk around with it still around him

Our *Hole One* our one for whom even perhaps
a divine annunciation might go
unnoticed though that seems
extreme and at least his
hole would then get flooded with supernal light

But I still hold out some
hope for him

that some multicolored butterfly or
thought might overtake him and overcome his
utter *holishness* before we have to

conclude it's his grave after all
and always has been

I pray that such a miracle occur

6/21

16 TEN SHORT REALITY CHECKS

1

One day something *unextraordinary* will happen
and we'll notice the difference between
it and what we have now and

be amazed

2

Hidden in the sound of a passing car
is an orchestra of camel caravans and
delicate machine factories even
farther away than Japan

3

The air that moves in this room from the
oscillating fan inflates the

room like a balloon that
rises over the city like a

setting sun

4

If at a signal all the doors in the world were simultaneously
closed and locked then would

there be peace on earth?

5

We have to have been brutes
to know how to kill like brutes

6

But all theologies deny it so it's maybe that
we've spent too much time watching
brutish behavior

7

I'm in the mood for love

8

If Allah took the veil away for
even one millisecond we'd be
shocked at the
simplicity of His Beauty

9

Little fungus shelf footholds in the woods
parasitically climbing all the way to the
top of a dead tree

10

If Allah took the veil away from
ourselves for just one millisecond

would we survive the vision of our
true glory or the sad truth of our ingrained

venality?

            6/24

17 NOAH'S MUSIC

Prophet Noah fell in love with rain

Its pounding on the ark roof struck his
heartbeats like a tuning fork

Its white watery streaks coming down from a
black sky womb in incessant sheets

The joy of all those aquatic animals and
water birds the silly penguins and
sleek torpedo seals and weasels

God's Voice-waves audible in lengthy water music
This absolute deed of His inundation visible

The heavens' rhythms and mirrored constant
bobbing under the boat's bow in cordial syncopation

Cascades spouting off the sides
out divinely inspired flues and drainpipes
like flared silvery wings

as he headed from one squall to
another down unfolding corridors of rainfall draperies
blacker than velvet toward no

certain light nor surcease of flood except what
he'd been promised and was

being promised with every rain-beat

His heart out there on the mast like
Odysseus's later ears stopped up and manacled past
the shipwrecking sirens' incessant magnetic song

But Noah's heart a tympani for
rain mallets hitting deeper sounds

Forty days and forty nights of aquatic fury
each drop a direct hookup to God's perfect purposes

Each animal eyeball in the dark trained on the
colossal chaos of water and yet
sweetly calm in their pure diurnal concentration

Noah at the helm letting
God be captain

Each driven drop that much closer to His
actual Action in the world

The shroud of sky itself an illumined birth canal
Noah's boat slid out of at last

washed utterly clean in
earth's new dispensation

remembering God's Names forever in the
hammering water drops and crashing waves'

compassionate collisions

                                                                       6/28

18 BUT WE KNOW BETTER

The sky is quiet tonight but we know better

The giant ship of death is behind it somewhere with a
famous ghost moaning at each porthole

(*There's Marie Antoinette holding out her head
to us*)

A green canopy of blessings for good harvests
A black canopy of drought or flood
for dearth's pernicious prominence

We know it contains the Four Horsemen of the
Apocalypse all fed and fresh to
blaze across the sky at a moment's notice

A celestial procession of officials in lavish
pomp and costume to stem a tide of
popular opinion or inaugurate a State

The quiet sky holding dark secrets
as well as light behind its neutral face

There's no "*arching over*" or "*inverted bowl of heaven*"
There's no "*Heavenly Mansions*" with iron gates
shut eternally against us newly padlocked

But love is there behind the quiet blankness

Great greased wheels of radiant acceptance of
everyone as we are with all our imperfections
ready to roll out across the heavens in a
giant steamrolling of God's Self-Actualization through our
own transparent negation in which we aren't
mowed down exactly but bob up again as pure spirit
with that spirit the spirit of love itself instead

There within the quiet sky
(*where last night was Qur'anic inundation*)

But just as easily Wrath's Engines could emerge
as they've enigmatically emerged before
creating no end of theological conundrum

but in the certain cycle of things
from which we all bob up again as before
praising on burnt or brilliantly lit lips
Him Who unleashes love and wrath equally
though He's promised love's unleashing way outstrips

Wrath's clumsy wagons
rattling over landscapes as in Heironymous Bosch
with bizarre wars raging against burning backdrops

Ah — here's a thunder rumble!
All's not as quiet as we think

Iron-booted though footless angels
walking sky's floorboards causing the
creaks to crack electrically overhead

either in dry storm or down-drenching rainfall

held back now but at the ready

behind the plugged-in twinkling

mother board of heaven

6/29

19 MONUMENTAL DAY

Today is a monumental day

I could build a bridge to eternity

or stand among my piles of paper perplexed

though to tell the truth I could still
build a bridge to eternity sorting through them

should a tall inaccessible tower of girdered light
stand inside this flesh mortal whose
own skeleton is such an elusive stalwart friend
there but hidden
as if behind a grove of shady trees

This minute is the key
and it plays the scales from high to
low and back again

and opens doors

Allah is never apart from us
even though we call on His Name

7/2

20 THE LATE MIDDLE AND EARLY PEOPLE

They told the late people they'd
erase all memory of the early people

They told the early people the late people
would never recollect them nor
what they did

The middle people were told they were
better than the early people and the
late people would experience a sudden
downfall

The late people began seeing signs of disaster
and tried to bring back the early people
through speculative archeology and
incantatory séances

The early people wanted to lay down the
foundations for every people to follow
so they perfected writing and
wrote like crazy

The middle people scoffed at their early
writings as unsophisticated though
philosophically interesting

The later people barely understood them at
all by piecing together flimsy lexicons based on an
imperfect inheritance of their language

Vague and mysterious things were attributed to
the early people by the late people but
the middle people were simply too busy
building on and deconstructing whatever it was
the early people were all about

Then there were the last people or at least
what latter people thought they were and
called themselves though there were

a number of people to go although it
looked both pretty grim and somewhat
conclusive what was going on with them
oblivious to the early middle and late people
hoping that by forgetting all about them
they'd supercede them or at least not be
tainted by their obvious failures
(obvious by the fact as they haughtily pointed out

that none of them survived nor were
apparently in existence except for a
few scant and totally unusable traces)

So we have the early people who actually
had some thoughts about the last people
and described them pretty accurately in their
odes and gnomic epics and ecstatic shaman utterances

And the middle people who really did do
everything middle as in "*middle of the road*"
"*middle child*" "*fair to middling*" etcetera and so

hoped to avoid both early and late
characteristics and yet had both

And the late people really only on the
cusp of being the "Last People" and they

thought too highly of themselves and their
increasing ignorance about people in general
both early and late except themselves

And the actual last people well they had some
enviable qualities and even occasional
humility in the face of it all

but they weren't in any way the last people
they were simply somewhere in the late middle

And Irene and Chester and the kids
lived as best they could from dawn to dusk in the
pocket of mortality they were given in the

opportunistic window span of their
lives through thick and thin and

neither oblivious nor slaves to early late or last
peoples' ways they hewed close to a

center as they knew it

And God looked at them with the
same Grace He gave everyone else wherever
they happened to trudge on the
human trajectory from

early to middle to late and last both
penultimate and ultimate

each breathing their entire allotment of
breaths and glancing at bird flight and
cloud cover as this jewel of a planet

gets continuously polished to a sheen and then

inevitably tarnished in its

incessantly unicyclic and swimmingly

circumferential rounds

                                                            7/3

21 HAIL THE EXPLORERS

Confounded by time and space never seemed to
worry the early explorers who kept
going through malaria and thirst parting

thick canebrakes and muddying their moccasins in
unfamiliar mud in order to

come out the other side and breathe air
never before breathed by let's say

white man or black man or whomever
was a newcomer here where white or
black or shades thereof may have been

living for eons never really bothering to see
what shook past yonder horizon the

cranes disappear over and the sun
sets below

Eating bugs or beetles roots or tubers
plants of such and such a feathery leaf
drinking water from such and such a
running source careful what might
lurk in its depths

Depending both on luck and blind faith
that past those bluish mountains over there
across that canyon through that gorge

the longed for idealized or at least
ideated territory of bright splendor lay
worth all this trekking

no yellow monster of snake-like imperturbable
gaze would spoil by raising its head out of
all that deepest unfamiliarity never before

seen by eyes of man or at least by

these explorers' eyes not having been
content to stare at the same four walls back home in
Kensington or Kent though the

velvet shirt get ripped to shreds and the
britches breached

No obstacle nor death nor greater disaster
can dissuade from the
forward march into God's private marsh

past whose perimeters the villagers might
look up one day and see this battered but

unbewildered band stumble in showing

signs of hunger and thirst while still
scribbling maps and asking incomprehensible questions
only the children seem to understand

                                                                                   7/11

22 PERSPECTIVE

A round window in a square wall
a square window in a round wall

Each adequate to look out of

onto a round world in a square universe
or a square world in a round universe

7/12

23 PROBLEMS OF TRANSLATION

They tried translating the fragment found in the
rubble from the original Ulgurik to modern Slambavik

but words resisted their efforts and
wriggled back into Ulgurik again leaving

bloody traces on the air

In a darkened back room men in T-shirts and all
wearing hammers in their belts were attempting to
translate a few lines of Smoojdarik into present-day
Jory so they could better understand their

ancestors' creeds but small electrical explosions kept

jolting them back and lighting up the original

shred in a way they couldn't understand

On a crowded street in the busiest
part of town a small bird-like woman was

attempting to pin down a few words in medieval
Falitch to find equivalents in

Dontatch so she could locate the early monastery's
ruins in the foundations of the new department store

A simple word like "*light*" or "*teeth*"

But in the new language the cluster of

elfish meanings is often absent and a
cricket walks across the page

chirping in its own tongue to the
deep satisfaction of a distant mate

7/14

24 SINGULAR SHADOW

A singular shadow stood on a road
and scratched its shadow head

wondering which road to go down
toward what shadowy goal

He tried to call out
but his voice was merely an echo

"*If I could only be more substantial*"
he thought to himself yet as the day waned
he became less so

He was shocked to see himself become
even more vague and indistinguishable

Some things like the imprint of tree branches as the
sun filtered down seemed to have
equal weight and some things like rocks
had more so

Yet he wasn't without life
certain things made him tremble slightly
though other things like the wind
didn't affect him at all

Where was he to go that was
different from where he came from?

And where was he now?

The road grew darker as the night came on

and he watched himself become
nothing at all

and the night become everything

7/15

25 SPHINX THOUGHTS

As I pull back the bedspread to sleep I
wonder if the Sphinx worries about its

disintegrating state that stately rough beast with
now broken nose and nearly faceless disappearing stature

who in its heyday posed impossible riddles and answered
serious questions but between French cannons fanatic
fundamentalists and Egyptian sands its pomp is now
poorer and its

pitiless stare less harsh on our human puniness

Though we might trudge to it full of Sphinxian zeal
and the way it rises from the ground still
has about it a certain cracked majesty
and its magnified size alone is still astonishing

Yet its pure stoniness empty of any living reality
now casts the longest shadow from its

prone bulk its extended paws almost
gone its haunches certainly not

now ominously grinding forward
in the sun-bleached sands

7/18

26 GREAT CRUELTY AND HEARTLESSNESS

We're living in a time of great cruelty and heartlessness
where instead of a sun they're throwing up
anvils

Instead of sunlight there's the sound of
hammers beating

Instead of walking there's kicking

Instead of thinking there's talking

It's almost as if there've never been times like
these before

Even shadows thrown by cartwheels on dirt roads
resemble the grimaces of armies as they
slide across rocks

In the palaces of power clocks go off but no one
wakes

Decisions are made by pouring acid down drains
or waiting for nightfall in a room lit by
neon tubes

If anyone speaks all eyes are upon them

I saw a sparrow fly over a fence

An ant stop and not go on

But laughter has turned to pebbles
falling on zinc

And children have been torn from their futures

7/19

27 WHAT BUGS WILL EAT ME

I wonder what bugs will eat me
when I'm in the ground

what worms and what they'll think of me

Choice delicacy? Will twittering antennae-gossip
travel round and gather them from

hill and vale wriggling or snip-snapping through
dark mud or green grass to reach me?

Hollow me out of all of myself down to the bone

as I've often wished in a way but never
would quite get at while alive at least not
to the bonework and its ichorous marrow

A grin will wreathe me
though I'd wish an aromatic feast impervious to their
jaws and mandibles

Probably their blind

eyes underground will make a ghostly
wreck of me

7/21

28 ANGELIC PHYSICS

The coolest part is in the center of a flame
The driest part is in the center of the sea

The highest part when the depths are home
The most healed part when all is broken

The whitest part when blackness surrounds
The quietest part in the middle of sound

The fastest part in absolute stillness
The sweetest part when bitterness obtains

and can't be shaken and horizons are
gun metal gray with one or two clouds

that move like camels with front legs hobbled
to slake their thirst at an oasis of openness

around whose perimeters angels are gathering
who'll soon appear in the vision of the most

hopeless among us at the very lip of despair

before all solace is foregone
in the gathering twilight lit by their

fiery dancing in the center of which is a coolness
in the drowning depths of which is a dryness

at the nadir of which is altitudinous light
that makes us whole out of uttermost brokenness

ignited in a night whose dark is hammering
but in the blast of each blow is serenest silence

whose stillness is such that it accelerates

a sweetness that pours out its

honeyed mouth into the world

7/22

29 THE ENORMOUS CORRIDOR OF SORROW

In the enormous corridor of sorrow

masked Napoleonic pygmies play with human
souls in the
shapes of coke bottles and guided missiles

and the clatter they raise
is more deafening than silence but

leads to the same end the same bolted door

A gigantic wheel rolls down
sorrow's enormous corridor aclattering

as if to challenge with grief its mere
invention as the era of slaughter

though it doesn't matter

I can't find my eyes among the rubble

A tsunami traded for the killer instinct in
the heart of man might set out a tea set
in the enormous tidal wave enough to

engender a pretense at civility though

no one finds himself more content
than the self-justified mass murderer

at home with his happy shadows

7/26

30 POLAR OPPOSITES

If I say *a white horse* do I mean
a black ship in the night?

If I say *the light played over the glassy lake water*
do I mean *like wool strangulation the dark
surrounded us*?

If I say *she bent to her task like a Siamese princess*
do I mean *he hacked down with his axe
like a Teutonic executioner*?

Words from our psyches on little wooden stilts
cross battlefields and the open plains
often meaning not what they say but rather
everything they don't say unless it's just
the opposite of what's said

So that *the deer on the hill looked majestically down*
might be *the uphill locomotive slowed in sheer exhaustion*

Or *he fell to the side after calling out to God
Whom he'd never before considered*
might be *he stood and greeted the
light that entered his room in response to his*

*usual prayer which he
knew one day would be answered*

7/28

31 BIRDS BURST INTO FLOWER

As she saw bombs burst into her backyard
she saw birds burst into flower

As he bit into the sandwich of death
he saw blazing armies of angels ride down a distant hill

As they played in a circle holding hands for the
last time the wide-eyed children felt a
geyser of silver light lift them into heaven

Rotors and rollers across house roofs and voices
became symphonic variations with bells and xylophones
in the ears of their dwellers

A scream took the shape of a blue phoenix
shot upward over a now desolate restaurant
in a golden display of unfolding fire in whose

heat vibrations you can see all the dead
in their prime getting ready for the
grand fiesta

Faced with no alternative
the cornered soap seller sang his favorite

aria from Verdi opening his vest button by button
and his mouth at last over a gulf of silence

The last bird out of the city
kept the sun on her right as she wheeled to a
nearby pasture

its light on her feathers
flashing an SOS to no one

Though God saw it
and exclaimed His Name to Himself
in the constant midst of our

mortal conflagration

                                                      7/29

32 LOVE EXCRUCIATING AS IT IS

In the midst of bomb blast
how can I raise my glass
to praise the Face of the one I love?

No tears nor beads of sweat no anguish
tortures its pure expression its moon-

light cast on cornfield equally as on
crash and catastrophic collapse on
bodies below as vulnerable as mine

Horses and grandmothers babies and bystanders
caught in the crush

Whole countries cracked up yet a bee nearby
gets pollen on its legs and buzzes home

Light fills my window same as Kabah wall and
Medina Tomb whose inner galactic glow showers
a ray out on the world that refuses its

healing balm or tortures it to
be what it's not

My loved one doesn't need my praise nor even
to be less inscrutable as usual in these

circumstances and still shows the way

So I say *"To this One there is no other*
(mother brother father sister)

None to claim us but proclaim us as
we proclaim in lifted liquor to our lips

our love excruciating as it is"

Yet a feather blown by it
floats in the air

and remains there

8/1

33 WORLD SPLIT APART

The façade of a building falls away and
reveals a man praying

A bakery loses its show-window showing a
hundred weddings who'll have to
wait in the next world for their cakes

An Orthodox cathedral split in two
revealing a solemn baptism that's now become
more like a drowning

A synagogue smashed like the tablets of Moses
the dust of the Torah continuing to
rise for years through the lunar cycles

A medieval mosque's minaret struck into rubble
and the muezzin's call going out bodiless
a hundred times louder

The road rutted with machinegun fire
and ghost cows dancing with their dazzled cowherds

New houses and old houses collapsing like cards
and the surprised furniture giving up their
inhabitants like birds released from their cages

Windows of government buildings falling into streets
revealing some making secret deals and others
receiving holy light for works of self-sacrifice
anonymously accomplished

A firehouse going up in flames and no
nozzle quenching it

A police department getting flattened and no
police whistles piping through the roar of falling plaster

Trees just coming into bud turning as black as
pokers their fruit both present and future
now gracing the fresh tables of the dead

Hillsides turning as black as ash
revealing lairs of tiny mammals
tremblingly shielding their young

This earth sliced apart like a unripe melon
revealing both incandescent fury
and radiant secrets of redemption
incomprehensibly intertwined

No one returning with a happy face at the
end of the day or followed by children like the
Pied Piper to safety beyond the rocks

The soul of man split asunder at the
first crack of unjust death and unjust retaliation

revealing a person naked drenched in
original water coming toward us surrounded by
anticipatory angels anxious for an

outcome already known to Him
who benignly created us

and Whose Voice rises inaudibly
above all other voices

saying over and over
the single word:

Peace

8/2

34 AN ANTELOPE GREW TIRED OF LOPING

An antelope grew tired of loping
and became a small thatched cottage on the
shady side of a hill where old people and

loving couples would pass by from time to time
and knock on the door and find
no one home

A lynx in the forest saw a slanting ray of sunlight and
became a dragonfly hoping to scale it to its
source and live daringly and un-lynx-like in its
bright delights above the earth forevermore

A stairway grew annoyed for the last time at all the
ups and downs ups and downs that went on and became a
prancing pony running free on hillsides of
buttercups and rhododendrons for one long
summer until it found itself taking
children around and around a corral which was
in any case better than being a staircase

And bankers became clouds and clergymen became
naked Roman statues and penguins remained penguins even
after given the opportunity of a lifetime to
leave the Antarctic once and for all

And we also in our constraints whistling to harmonize with
shrill factory let-out or a Broadway orchestra or
the latest pop song

somehow bursting out of our solitary confinement from
time to time to knock on the

door of a little thatched shack on the
shady side of a hill and find
no one's there that bounds off behind us

to be an antelope again joining its
nervous herd able at a

flick of an ear or tail to take off like a shot

as one beast singularly and explosively bursting with

fear and boundless joy

            8/5

35   BUG GRATITUDE

> The little bug I coaxed onto a card and
> then put out the door
>
> probably didn't know what hit him
> though in my mind he said "*Thank you*"

8/10

36 FLOWER OF LANGUAGES

There's the elaborate stem of the flower in a
kind of nest of radiant feathers

whose fibrous tuber is made up of the
strands of all languages known since the

world began threaded out in a kind of
angelic disorderly wire-recording of speech

now lost forever among the rocks and pines

And the lowest leaves are first inklings of prophetic
light the first slow movements sunward

and above them are leaves in prophetic glory
actually singing back to the sun their

chlorophiliac gratitude in serrated edges and
crispily folded surfaces from central vein outward

The stem proceeds upward in actual ascension
while this poem is being written it

rises almost imperceptibly but continuously
and as it does so it expands past horizontal dimension

to include parts of our lives whose
consciousness has retreated back into shadow

But this stalk or stem or slim verticality
lifts the world as it lifts itself

as we see what our state gives us to see
and sing out what stanzas we

have been given to sing

as the stem continues rising to its crown
whose rotations galactically strew their

pinkish rays across distances beyond measurement
in which only the Eye of Wisdom is

able to fathom both the
illimitable as well as the effusively flowering limits

           8/11

37 SERPENT IN THE PLUMBING

There's a serpent named Death
who lives in the plumbing

and no amount of water
will wash it down

We can only see the flick of its eyes from
time to time
by looking down

or hear its hiss especially from the
pipes of others

Though our plumbing not be long
inside our fragile frames

we feel it goes on and on
as long as the ocean
of its source or final outlet

Sunlight eternal on its ripples
whales in its deeps and
dolphins on its waves

Though it be but pipe
a few feet long

and inside it coils
that serpent taking its shape
no matter how many coils

flicking its eyes and tongue unseen
in ourselves

though we only seem to
know it for sure

from others

8/15

38 THE ELVES HAVE TAKEN THE EARTH AWAY

The elves have taken the earth away
and put a hard black ball in its place

And as sticks fly and balls careen across the green
everyone's supposed to quietly drink their milk?

While we're *on* one of them?

And they've taken the leaders away
and replaced them with nefarious smoke-screens in
man-and-woman shape whose lips are out of
sync with what they say

and what they say is creels full of eels!

And they've carted *us* away

And put one mouse one heifer one blasted
barn about to topple over one steamship one
blue ribbon and one white
and several pins of no use to anyone

and expect these to get along better than
we did and they
probably will
(*especially the pins*)

They've carted language off in small carved wooden blocks for
every sound letter vocable trill and word ever
used on earth so that now
instead of the Tower of Babel we have

almost no speech left to us at all

so we must learn love's body language
quick before they take that away as well

But they'll never take that away

ah no they'll never take *that* away!

              8/19

39 THE ARROW

An arrow that left its bow in the Middle Ages
is still in orbit round and round the

earth not having found its target
flying straight ahead in the throes of Zeno's

Paradox in time and space
its dark feathers intact

passing over the heads of us all and
looking down as it speeds past

thinking to itself *"How sad they've become
with their bombs and technology*

*We'd shoot to kill and then it's done
bad enough but nothing like*

*what they do now at the
flick of a switch"*

8/20

40 HE RACES TO THE EDGE

He races to the edge only to find
the edge is in himself

She rises to the top with psychic corpses piled below her
only to find a new dimension starts with her and
she's at the bottom

They takes sides only to discover their own
sides have been squeezed into a middle

He reaches rock bottom only to see he's
at the top of an inverted pyramid with
gold clouds round his head

All this by Allah
Who is not a wind caught in an elevator

nor a rainbow arching over a suspension bridge

nor the thought that passes through a murderer's
mind that stays his hand

nor the song that leaps to the mute's lips

nor the sight that fills the blind's eyes

nor the soothing call that enters the deaf's ears

when we have all awakened out of our
slumber of soot and clay

but the Name within a name whose
elegant articulation

lifts things finer than gnat's wings
into the air

and lifts the air itself repeating it more
deeply than space repeats itself to itself and

then to all other

sister brother father mother

8/21

41 SEISMOGRAPH

A seismograph is placed on his heart
and the earth trembles

There are so many people under its lid as if
down in a bunker huddling
everything from babies to frying pans and
buildings toppling over

He balances a tea tray on his head and the
sugar cubes leap in the air

If the earth were only in less of a hurry to
shake us off do you think?

And where could we go?

Is there a place of greater peacefulness?

Rollers on gravel tracks
make a noise like the night
getting out of itself through a very small
hole

And back into itself when we

open our eyes and find we're in a
flutter of feathers

more alone than alone

longing to be alone *with* The Alone

8/23

42 DEATH'S DOOR

At death's door
one knock is all it takes

Though a song is always better
to make its hinges glow

And a shout of joy makes the
grain in its wood grow

into a meadow

8/23

43 I SANG

I sang in the dark of the single cell

and in the splendor of the trillion-celled gargantuan
crossing a black lake

and in the many-armed and the no-armed
I also sang

and in the sunrise in liquid form
and in the sunset when liquid sets hard as night

and over the stout field my song's been heard
as well as remote at sea in a trireme of billows

I sang among leapings and divings
singing at the top of my lungs

There's no one singing when I sing
for I do not sing for myself

but for the dot aloft among the dotless

or the splurge of leaflets littering the longitudes

A voice heard above other voices or the

blend of them all in unreachable registers

And I sang before when all was silent
and will sing again without pause after this brief

respite though this also is song

And death looks kindly on such singing
through eyes that have never been endured before

like two high burning campfires

on a black hill

8/23

44 THE LIGHTHOUSE WIDOW'S PRONOUNCEMENTS

"Out the window is a window

and in that window is another window"

said the widow folding her late husband's sail
into increasingly small fourths as the

waves crashed below

"and in those waves are other waves

and in their crashings are other crashings"

her cracked face crinkling as she winced against

the sun

"There's no end to endlessness" she said

and we both sat in her lighthouse and agreed

"though endlessness be shorter than you think"

and she gave a wink

"*much much shorter than you think*"

I saw planets line up in the sky

and marveled at their brilliancy

"*shorter than you think*" she said

"*much much shorter than you think*"

                                                                        8/25

45 THE TURNING

The attorney in the wide black coat turned
and the chef in the tall white hat
and the ballet dancer in fluted pink tulle
and the sword swallower in tight striped jacket
also turned

And the pancake seller in his rainbow shirt
and the school children in identical charcoal jumpers
and the parrot trainer nude to the waist and the cobbler
all turned at almost the same moment

And the steamship captain in his buttoned blue jacket
and the retired cowboy actor in shaggy vest
and the contralto in her loose work clothes
and the hardware salesman in Levi overalls

They all turned at the sound of the surprise downbeat
with no words on their lips

And we made our way through the crowd that had
also turned in one unanimous motion
toward what it was we were all
turning toward

And the blundering ex-Prime Minister of an ex-colonial
power in his pajamas and the present Undersecretary of
External Affairs with name tag in brass on his blue serge lapel

And the head of the local Rose Society in her
expensive Paris rose-colored gown turned as if toward the
arrival of an important guest

And the author of sea adventures in turtleneck turned
and the young woman stenographer in mini skirt whose
future was uncertain

And none who turned at that precise
moment could be certain why they turned exactly
though the turning was instinctual and precise

the explosion of light not confined to the
horizon each sought with their eyes
but also surprisingly arising within them
believe it or not
so that as if on a pivot all turned at
once and as one toward it

The most hoped for ideal achieved in that moment
all differences erased no matter by

stiff celluloid collar or loose paint-spattered smock
high cheekboned or hooded steely-staring

each of us turned before our

actual deaths to the anvil strike of that which we
all have always hoped for in pleasurable harmony and

perfect recognition of hallowed radiance
on all our souls at once

toward which we will all
as one

most gratefully

turn

               8/26

46 LOOKING AND SEEING

The hardwood trees knocked to see if He was there
and He replied
but He was not there

And the rainfall straight down sought Him
and He Spoke
but He was not where they were

And the fires reached skyward to find Him
with their snaky fingers and His Voice could be
heard entwining among them
but He was not
where embers lay

And oceans rolled and rerolled endlessly seeking
His pleasure and He assured them and their
punctual surfs
but He was not among them

And dolphins dove and heard His dolphin laughter
but He eluded them

And falcons looked with beady eye and heard His
breathing in the wind
but He was not confined

And we look and listen exhort and even
try to command
and in filters the texture of Him from time to time
when our hearts burst with it
or our minds reach their
natural limits

But He is not there in a
there sense
and He is not elsewhere in an
elsewhere sense

Lifting the arm off the record doesn't silence Him
though He did not speak

And yet His
Word was Spoken

Just as this world is His and Him though it
seems only a token of what
He is

And He is here
but you might not know it

though His traces leave traces that
openly show it

8/27

47 CAMPING TRIP

"We're all on a camping trip see

only instead of a tent we've brought a body

and instead of tent poles we've brought

bones

Look at the moonlight

through the trees!"

8/28

48 DOT

If life begins in a dot smaller than a
blemish on your little finger

in a cosmos of universes in which earth is smaller than
a dot the size of a blemish on your
little finger

which itself could be contained in a drop of water the
size of a dot smaller than a blemish on your
little finger

which sits on a tiny glass table in a
chamber so filled with light it's like
angelic laughter

that lasts a billion years which in total time is like one
small chuckle less than a blip on a

screen the size of a dot smaller than
a blemish on your little finger

and we raise our heads once in
arrogant pride or stand with feet spread
as if trees should bend to us

then that burp you heard a second ago
was all this in concentrated form

to question by an abrupt explosion of air
our existence less than one intake or

outbreath of that air as an unreality unworthy
of notice except that we're also

reflections of He Who is the One Reality in
all this

And thus it all matters however minute it
may be in the totality of things which is

also He Who is the One Totality of that
totality and the only One

worthy of
worship

9/4

49 SEED

In the Botanic Garden the potted beauties
clamored to be released

so I took a seed

9/5

50 WHAT THEN?

Everything is where it should be
and the water runs out the faucet nicely

but what about when it isn't
and the water no longer flows

and the squirrel doesn't run across the
telephone wire out back with
no sign of nervousness

and the plants in the garden out back so
beautifully catching the rain and sunlight
and beaming back sheer beauty

and the sky clears then clouds then
clears again with robin's egg shades of blue

But what about when it doesn't anymore
and no cloud appears and no mist evaporates
and everything is eerily still

without even mentioning those live shots of
dead planets we've seen lately taken by our
immensely expensive and successful

robot cameras orbiting further away than
anyone but saints and theologians could
see clearly or prophets describe in detail before
the placement of things here in the room
around me and that I'm also placed around

when it's gone and filtered out through
yard sales and flea markets like the
diced cloak of Jesus or Scrooge's bedchamber items
fought over by desperate street urchins

and our breaths and eyeblinks so nicely natural
now and coming with Swiss regularity

and the dependable jazz band of heartbeats and
pulses throughout the body like an
athletic modern dance troupe going through their
gravity-defying choreography and
formal horseplay in big loops and leaps

Where will all that go when it is no longer?

The itch I've just lifted pen from paper to
scratch just southwest of my neck on my
very palpable shoulder with its
scritchy-scratchy sound

and the airplane full of passengers now heard
on its lifting trajectory over Philadelphia

*Where will it go when it no longer
comes or goes?*

These fragile thoughts stretched between
one point and another like spider webs that
get dewdrops in glistening spangles
and are known for their strong resilience
but then are suddenly gone and the spider's moved on

And this chug chug of questioning when there's
no fuel or track left and even the
strange space it's in has vanished?

What then?

9/8

51   THE ISLAND

That island among the chain of islands
down there

surrounded by bright turquoise water lapping
round it like a frame around a picture

and the smoke clouds or mist clouds that
dot-dash their way above it down there
so that it always has a Morse Code commentary
vapor teletape mentioning the weather or more
mystical things which as we can't possibly

read it we'll never know as they drift their puffy way across
just as we'll never know for sure exactly

who carved the somber anonymous statues
each with a particular gesture some of

refusal it seems and some of humble submission
though no other human artifacts have been

found in conjunction with any of them
and the current language spoken by every
inhabitant of this island is pure silence

Even the crickets are quieter here out of
some either acknowledgment of sanctity or

lack of will to sing their lovesick songs
and the dry grasses and gorgeous wild and eccentric

orchids here that abound each with a
kind of face on it which upon

closer inspection is the actual faces of each of ourselves looking
back at us almost as clearly as in a

mirror and I mean every living person on
earth at the time has a face on these

fiery and snowflake-like orchids growing out the
side of a giant shale hill above a

deep gorge of distant thick darkness
that seems to go down to the

very center of the island and perhaps even
further

9/9

52 THE CAT'S GONE MAD

This time it seems cat's gone mad
the saucepan's full of Eiffel Towers
the moon's a light bulb in the sky
the song is sung by hothouse flowers

who've lived their life of luxury
in perfect temperature control
but now the shoe is on your head
and now the body is the soul

I really wish I could see clearly
the end of night and all its roses
the train is coming through again
the discus thrower's dropped his poses

and shown he's really the FBI
puts on his clothes and drives away
I wish I'd known this all before
so I could know just what to say

A horse leaps higher than the fence
a fox is hiding in the lettuce
God's love pours down through every tree
I wonder why it just can't get us

back on track the way we were
when we saw past stars and planets
but something shadows in between
stronger than a giant magnet

I insist again that light be shed
in every little nook and cranny
before the jelly all turns green
and they start again to call me Danny

The earth's a colossal megaphone
to broadcast all our hopes and fears
so let's praise God with every
ounce of strength in our remaining years

9/11

53 AND OF THE LITTLE THAT WE DO

God of the dew and the dew's disappearance
of the pelican walking a pier and the
next day's tsunami
of a face caught in a window and the
window's blankness and blackness one second later

God in Whose invaluable Presence we rely without
seeing You though I've always contended the
orbs of sight through which we see are
proof of You beyond refutation

And into Whose Presence we call on to be
absorbed just as shadows are drawn into both
light and darkness without objection

And how both light and darkness are absorbed
in each other alternatively without objection

And how a crash of cymbals gradually
dies away until one struck note of the
heavenly celesta is audible again

And hoof prints like zippers in the snow over the
hill disappear both in thaw and in more sheets of snowfall

And of pain and its gradual ceasing in
both directions
toward relief or toward the sheer snowfall of totality

There's a garden out back in the night now
but I know what's growing and the
riot of color however silent it remains

And the silent multitudes of people whose
mouths are sealed with fear or forbearance
waiting for You to remove their seals personally

like a wine merchant readying his
products for sale knowing how perfectly they've aged

This poem is going nowhere but to You
God of an earth whose epiphanies are
ceaseless and constitute a
continuum

Who's at ease in the knowledge of the
exact shape of the cosmos as if it were a
small sculpture on a table in front of You which You
take up to observe more closely

O God of all this
and of all that we
don't know

and of the little that we do

                                        9/13

54   RIDDLED WITH BULLETS

I've never quite understood the phrase
"riddled with bullets"

since at that point
the riddle seems to be

solved

9/14

55 I SHOULD BE ASLEEP

I should be asleep
but smolder from the burning city keeps
passing a smoke-film across my eyes

and the newly drowned keep calling out
from the river

The horses have broken free from their stables
and run in all directions then regroup and
run as a wild herd again
illuminating the hills and valleys with their
fierce beauty

The bridges are all on fire though and the
glow pours a strange light along the
house fronts and low clouds

Birds cry across the darkness and babies seem to
answer them from behind their fuzzy windows

Someone called out to God and the others
cursed him

Someone else drove his car through the wreckage hoping to save himself but

falling girders prevailed

There must be a way out besides sleep

but I'll probably choose sleep after all

and wake refreshed in the morning

                                                                               9/17

56 SONG OF DEPARTURES

We all must have our song of departures

for when the long shadow down the road we're on
coming from in front of us

catches up with us

and covers us like an amorous lover
from head to toe with sultry kisses

then we know we're going where
all caps are worn backwards

and every window looks in rather than out
at the world

Pools reflect more than sky with clouds overhead
they also show our watery roots
and the purification of our desires for
One Beloved alone out of Whom

all others fan and into Whom all collapse back again
singing to us their own song of departures as they

slide into His Single Sovereignty after all

There's a tree here
that would also like to beckon us goodbye
and it has rainbows around each leaf
and faces in the shadows of everyone we've

ever known but as it's the tree of life it has for
each of us only faces each one of us

has truly known yet they're all the same Face
and sing their own song of departures among the
leaves as they fall or as they blossom
each spin of the cycle we're in

slowly saying goodbye to it all

So slowly at first we're not saying goodbye
at all but hello and every

conversation in between

But each is a departure

And each is a song

9/18

57 SHADOW MAN

I wasn't there the day shadow man came to
town but I heard he made quite a stir

People stopped and gawked though there was
nothing to him you could put your finger on

No smile no blue eyes no descriptive scars
just an outline a shape as fragile as a skyline

He sauntered in and walked down every street
sat in every chair and looked at every ledger

that made the townsfolk uneasy but even more
his lack of reaction his sublime disinterest though he

intently bent to each task he undertook
and no one was absent from his suave scrutiny

Then he got up in one liquid motion
and slid out between things as silently as he'd arrived

And there are two kinds of people now
those who won't talk about it

and those who can't stop talking about the
day shadow man came to town

and ran his breath over everything and some said
took all the luster out of things

while others said he brought things into
sharper definition and clearer perspective

The radicals among the townspeople tried to
contact him to come back and let himself get

known more intimately while the
conservatives while pretending approval with a

kind of starched nonchalance were actually
scared silly he might do just that

But one visit is enough and only rarely does he
make two but the impact is deep and

no one remains quite the same after
shadow-man comes to town

9/22

58 BONE

There in the graveyard

no one brings their "*knickknack*"

No one brings their "*paddywack*"

But everyone brings their "*bone*"

9/25

59 PILLARS OF CLOUD

Pillars of cloud extend down to earth
during Ramadan

inside of which angel coils swirl continuously upward and
downward to a sweet music just beyond

earshot

Great aerial pulleys and gears mistily squeaking like
crickets calling out for mates in their

emeraldine solitudes

And great transparent columnar tubes amplifying distant voices
and inside the voices meanings in incomplete

sentences

The intermingling of sounds and voices
completed by our hunger for His sake

And then our palatial appreciation of any morsel that
breaks it as if such hunger

never existed

9/26

60 FRAGILE SCATTERING BEADS

At the edge of a piece of blank blue-lined paper
where strange suns rise and set
casting a green glow on words unwritten

suddenly a space appears out of which
I would like to entice a smoke that becomes
a city or a person or small

mammal on its way somewhere to hide or
retrieve food or find refuge in
high branches or deep burrow

and shafts of light spraying up from
some grotto in the earth as if to entice us to
follow them down to caverns where the

treasure's been waiting all these centuries to be
found

But we pass it by out of oblivion or cowardice
unable to let ourselves down one of those
shafts past any darkness we might encounter to

rocks high almost as the wheeling gulls themselves
against whose stalwart towering crags

century after century great thunderous waves crash and
explode

into fragile scattering beads

9/26

61 STARTING WITH SEVEN ELEGANT COWS

I

Seven elegant cows sauntered into a barn
and transformed themselves into seven
hooded monks heading for glory

They left on a sunbeam without even one blade of
straw trampled and walked along a lake

singing tunes to make both townspeople and
catfish swoon
as squirrels stand at attention paws at their
chests in sudden recognition

One monk's face was a wheel of cheese
one monk's face was a rugged sunlit hill
one monk's face looked always askance or even
further away into mirrors of blue clouds
one monk's face had a vaguely bovine look
one smiled more sunnily than the sun herself
one was often in the Lord's Presence for his
eyelids fluttered with moonlit purples and the
far screams of peacocks in scraggly trees

And the seventh monk unshaven and alone
was their leader in daring and striving
who turned simple things complex and
unraveled complexities by simply lifting one
finger as if all light had its primal origination at its

tip

2

The miraculous doesn't really seem that
farfetched when you think of it

A globe of water and ice dirt and fire
suspended in an orbit swimmingly in space
like a tossed rock that never lands

and all the strange things on it with
open mouths to gulp in air or wiggling
hairs to navigate through tiny fluid passageways

make flying through space by simply tilting
one's head or touching with fingertips a
row of stones and they turn into perfect
croissants not all that spectacular in fact

Or that such light should flow out of one or two
mortals who illuminate our total path from
birth to death with sublime elocutions in
linguistic detail reverberating in the
hearts of everyone pro or con for all eternity

nothing short of miraculous as much as
dandelion filaments with seed anchors
floating to new fruition or that

slippery worms know where to go deep down in the
loam to fulfill their most elegant essential worminess

makes our seven hooded monks turning back and
forth into farm implements or rows of
rosewater in cobalt glasses on a
sick boy's windowsill or crows

landing in Van Gogh's field to warn him of
death an almost absurdly simple violin note held

indefinitely on a single string on the
violin of The Miraculous held

lightly by God's untrembling bow across

the entire heavens and in each of our

hearts held together as one by its

multi-vibrational tone

62 AT THE HOUSE OF THE LORD

At the House of the Lord of Creation
no one is served just bread or just wine
in goblets the shape of our lives on taller
stems

No one is divided in two
but we are all invested with the
power of song and the words are
given to us in silver ewers and the
melodies are served to us by silver tongs
and they come effortlessly together
and create rolling hills of windowsills in

whose frames we see all lives as
our own and our own as
nothing but anonymous forward motion
in shades of green

At the House of the Lord of Creation
we pass the night and go instead
into crystalline areas where we
see voices as ferns in
various stages of unfurling growth
and the highest boyish voices are

the darkest while the deepest bassos
are sparkling moist elocutions of light

At the House of the Generous Host we're
asked to want anything and
everyone is baffled

And that bafflement is His gift to us
direct

And the bread is stampeding herds in snow in
all directions and the wine is our

goblets in the Prophet's moonlight shed on
the hills where the stampede takes place

And no one is dissatisfied with such an
outcome

And no one asks if things could be
explained any more clearly

           10/4

63 THE HEART KNOWS

The heart knows what the mind
doesn't know

or some say
the heart knows what the mind

can't know

10/5

64 THE CREATOR'S GLITTERING HIEROGLYPH

Maybe as you get older pain builds little
colonies of clustered muscle and bunched nerves

to align the well-aged body with that of the earth
volcano-pocked and crater-cracked with its

utter shelves and drops its dips and giveaways

so generously but perilously extended in
sunlit and ever sun-baked display

now evident in my body for example
tossing and turning on mattress and head

bunched into pillows looking for the soft repose
sweet sleep and its canoe adrift forever

so much perhaps like our more final repose among the
rocks and hardness of earth itself when we'll

not so much feel anymore as
decay around our feelings exposing unless

true sanctity preserve us the chalky whiteness at the

stony heart of our bodies the long femur flutes and
ribbed xylophones then silent in a sweet

God-blessed sleep painless as flight itself
though beyond my grasp tonight alive and

achy in places I'd not felt achy before
my brash sixty-six years in the body-wrapped organ loft

playing on all the keys the most high-
piping music to passing clouds and

heavenly wisps in a body of earth God Himself
breathed into after pinching mud and dirt and

fine singing clay piece by piece into shape
more cunning than anything previously known on

earth and now with minor pains turning into
earth itself feeling the mortal pinch as much as

rift or schist or glift or cliff of ocean's theft of
the Creator's glittering hieroglyph

                                                          10/6

65 FLAKES

We live in a world full of dust and bits
phlegm-splats and piss-squirts

Buddhist monks make much of sweeping
and polishing the mirror clean

How do we do it? Go through such a flitty
debris-floating world with its various
scums and sooty surfaces? Breathing some of it
deep in and exhaling some back out in

little invisibly wriggling devils lost in the dim?

Hair full of flakes but similar flakes falling
everywhere

Ourselves a falling flake with His
Face on it

10/6

66 TIME'S WHEEL

Time moves like a big stone wheel over
uneven ground
dipping into gullies then righting itself forward
another crunch

It sits in a windowsill in a glass thimbleful of perfect
claret the sun shines through tempting
trembling lips with its color of sweet drowning

Why do we tolerate its expansion or else its
dilapidation? Its

running forward or its running down?
All things "growing older" from a primal

starting point though each moment is also an

island with its own sly vegetation and inhuman
yowls of wild beasts hungry for our
aging flesh rejuvenated down the

windy road

We are one with it

We put our hands around our own necks
to measure it

As long as we sing it continues its
calculations and when we fall silent it's the

stone wheel again so slowly crushing toy boats and
work boots in its path though there's

no reversing it

Allah sits on the Throne of it

He's in control of it

its mercy and its

deathly thrills

10/10

67 WRITTEN IN THE DARK AT THE FEZ MUSIC CONCERT

for Mahmoud Ayoub and Lena

What we do for love!

The rhinoceros turns into a sparrow and
eats seed

The river runs vertically to become a
building housing those in need

The preposterous propositions of
daylight become interludes of lunar
sweetness by night

The charades and double-crosses of
public life become unashamed openness
in a purple darkness

The worm forgives the plow but the
plow also forgives the harsh sky
and miles of fallow fields left barren

Because what we do for love
we won't do for anything else
or anything less

Nothing would stop the avalanche
from tumbling upward

The locomotive from becoming a hillside of
sheep softly chewing

Hands from everyone on earth
taking hold of each other in a
loving gesture circling forever

Or musicians who've never
played together before from becoming

a road to infinity bordered by

perfectly symmetrical telephone
poles as far as the

eye can see

                                                     10/10

68 ULTRA SHORT EDDA

1

He took his coat his hat and his antlers
and put them on out the

door into the howling tundra on little
deer's feet those cloven "V's" in

snow that lead you right to them against
all that whiteness witnessing

one of the wonders of the world the sheer
extent of so much landscape to such

blaring trumpets of cold and brazen iciness

2

What we didn't know or couldn't
see in all that glare

was the doe of silvery stillness beyond the
farthest edge whose dew-sweat sheath

kept her secret except to her lovers
and they were tuned in to it like

radar across whatever distances
as she patiently awaited one to

simply arrive
as he loped closer down the

busy avenues of cities and towns
mythic in his hugeness and his

animal shadow cast against each
setting sun and each of its risings

3

Their union on the ice
lowers the eyes

The light from it
radiates suns

Glorialis aurora borealis
shivers its sights

across the ice
in His Majesty's Light

10/14

69 BEARD

for Michael Hannon

As his poems grew shorter
his beard grew longer

until it trailed behind him
as he walked

When his poems finally got to
one word

he was wrapped in it
and buried under the floor

10/18

70 PERFECT TINY BLUE ROSE

for Malika

I

My shambly camel trudges down the alleyway
looking for a water trough

Or my ichthyic fish gapes its scaly mouth
deeper than darkness making O's but no
sound

Or somewhere a window goes up to let out a
fly whose life has just been extended a few
wing beats more

Or a gate post falls southward in a
high wind and a hundred white goats traipse free
eating grass they only spied from a
distance before

All these events related only by the atomic
principles of their creation the very fact of
their being as well as my

pauper's mind seeing them come to a kind of
life under my pen this night of

Ramadan possibly *Lailat al-Qadr* with the

soft patter of rain outside and me up
at 2:30 a.m. much later than anticipated

No sound in the house but the ticking of clocks

No sound on earth but life ticking and its
hands moving inexorably forward

And saintly eyes wider than their sockets or
their physical orbits watching us with
sweet compassion and amusement or

sweet amusement and compassion

As we roll giant hoops over rocky ground or

leap over a stick and think we're Superman

or stand as tall as possible in our bodies
while draping cloth-like flags to hide our
Edenic nakedness in the dwindling light

And over all God's peace that comes dropping slow
in boats rowing and long winding hedgerows

across this merrily rotating earth happy in its
mighty ermines as well as in its daily minks

twinkling like any other star

2

A perfect tiny blue rose falls into place in the
buttonhole of the bridegroom's lapel

as I grow older than cinders and am
blown up flues and out into the world

from the rosy red hearth of God's living heat
inside all living things happy or unhappy about our

daily and nightly mortal predicament
looking out the bars of our cage

The first dawn is still filtering through the trees
and the first shout of love is still

ringing in our ears

The first sight of you naked under the first

waterfall in gold shimmering light
and the first word ever spoken still

sizzling on our tongues no matter what grammatically
complex language we speak

Firstness and lastness come together like
a rainbow arc over a desolate island in the Pacific

Or in the eyes of the great-great-great grandmother of us all
who for all we know is exactly the

same one

We're all out on a limb here
reaching for the furthest-most apple

We're all sitting in God's shadow
waiting for His loving reply

10/19

71 IN THE AIR AND ON EARTH

Our son's in the air from Zurich via London
as I'm stretched out on the couch reading
poems and thinking when he
comes in the door it'll be as if he was simply

teleported from nowhere to here in the flesh
coming out of a black hole to take form among us on earth

though we've heard his disembodied
voice on the telephone and seen his

hologrammic face on IChat still it's
another thing altogether to actually

see him walk in the door in the flesh fresh from
an exhausting Atlantic air crossing dozing and
waking under a thin blue airplane blanket or putting his

tray up for takeoff or landing or getting up to
wobbly thread down the aisle past bald or hairy sleepers and

late novel readers to slip into the airplane bathroom pulling
the strange accordion door clicking closed behind him

all the while we on earth going about our
business or sleeping ourselves on our

stationary beds on a planet that's also careening many

miles an hour through space all of us in the

flesh all of us disembodied all of us God's

holograms grinning at each other

through the front door of arrival's

first dawning light

                                              10/20

72 JOB WAITED BY THE DOOR

1

Job waited by the door for a change of heart

It didn't come

What came were detractors to
convince him otherwise
and curse the darkness

But there was a door in the darkness
and Job waited there for a change of
heart that would pry it open

He could see the sheep-clotted meadow beyond it
and the singers under the tree with
lutes and harps and could

almost hear their music and
make out their words

He waited for the good sound to hit his ears
the rustling of grass the buzz of gnats in
sheep's wool the sound of

sunlight hitting sunlight

We're waiting with him here with our
scabs and wounds and pottery shards

knowing there's a door in the darkness

waiting for the change that will pry it open

2

Break the tooth on the broken board
and the brow on the boat hull

The heel on the claw and the clay of light
and the shaped shard of a seed husk raw

as regeneration in its mess and muster
as it sails forth to the central water

a dot in the great pond gathering its mastery
against mass slaughter

where it really matters

in the mouth of the master and the
mother of masters

its hallowed daughter

10/23

73   WHAT THE TABLE HOLDS

The sketch left on the table of the active volcano
starts smoldering and out of it pours

the hot viscous stuff that drowns villages and
burns a swath through anything it finds

And the book left on the table of the great
battles of the civil war bursts into two

ragtag factions hiding in a New England woods
shooting their rifles into the mist at each

other with occasional raw teenagers cursing and
falling over

And the postage stamp on the letter on the table
with the tropical parrots on it suddenly

applauds into squawks and flutterings of
parrot pairs crisscrossing the room whose

temperature has precipitously risen

so that to know is to see that indefinable
linkage between the indicator and the

indicated and roses bloom in the pages of
magazines in doctors' and dentists' offices

And elephants trumpet in schoolroom
National Geographics until you can

really smell pachyderm dust back there among the
greenish aquariums and hamster cages

And if we say God God's near and if we
love God hearbeatingly God's closer still

And this gets both subtler and harder to
articulate as we get closer and closer to

that which we love and desire above all
He Whose pronoun becomes present in its

absence and absent in its presence as
the room fills with light the same light that

fills the universe coiling and tumbling
end-to-end here and everywhere at once

amen

    10/24
    ('Eid 2006)

74 WHEN THERE'S NOTHING TO SAY

When there's nothing to say
it says itself

And silence is the cap worn by
the loquacious in a room gone dark

filled with tomorrow's dust
off the main corridor where

dancing can be heard
in the main hall

of sleepless revelers
who need no sleep

who clap hands at the Name of God
and whose eyes have been exchanged

for God's Eyes

though you'd never know it to
look at them

Their silence is sound and
their sound silence

Their steps are not their steps
and their breathing circular

And the circle goes on without us
and they know it

And it goes on around us
with or without us

though you can't hear it

here in the room gone dark
off the main corridor

where revelers call on His Name now
in silence

                                                    10/27

75 THE SHAPE OF THE ROSE GARDEN

for Omar Tufail

The rose garden's in the shape of a rose
that fits nicely into your buttonhole
so that everything around you is leaves and stems

and as you walk petals fall

And the shape of the roof of your house
is the shape of the roof of the world
a veritable Lhasa of bells and
turning drums that tell prayers into the air

And the shape of your heart is your outward and
inward shape over desert stretches and
canyon deeps calling out among echoes
for the right response

And the night with this pattering rain
is the perfect diamond shape
that brings light and peace within
a kind of faceted crackling reach

And the shape of a water drop is the shape of
all the heavens it's come from
and we might see our reflection in it

as it falls to earth to seep
into the ground to evaporate again

to a point beyond sense
the home of us all

from which all the drops of us
have come

10/28

76 A SPARK IN YOUR BEING

A light on the horizon expands to
become the horizon

A sip in the glass expands to
become an ocean enough to
slake everyone's thirst

A path becomes a road and you
find you are on it and
heading for the goal of it before

the whole forest burns and
encroaches upon it

The terrible burning that
encroaches upon everything

Though a spark in your being expands
until you're a flare
a torch lighting
everything entirely

and no one is exempt from
the light that you shine

10/30

77 TWO

Two men went out

One caught a big fish
One caught a tin can

One caught a lovely wife
One caught the clap

One came back dressed in name brands
One came back dressed in a sheet

One's name means quality
One's name brings low guffaws

One sailed the high seas
One's face down in rain

One heard the call and sang
One mocked the call and died

11/1

78 DON'T FORGET CHUMLEY

Three to play and Chumley don't forget Chumley

And we'd meet outside by the garden wall
the three of us and Chumley
one tall as a beanpole one down low to the
ground and one mean when startled

And we could hear voices over the wall
the three of us and Chumley
who insisted on coming so OK you can
come this once Chumley but

always it was Chumley

And the voices and wailing and hollering
over the wall made us stop made us
change our plans there was

something so awful and human or inhuman
about those voices as we four

the three of us and Chumley

crouched close to the wall listening until
every other sound disappeared except the

breathing of the three of us and of course

Chumley

Something was going on as usual there but
each time it fascinated us and made us

fearful and elated at the same time somehow
made us listen harder than we'd
ever listened and quieter than we'd

ever been quiet in our lives until then
all four of us

the three of us and Chumley

And then it was Chumley who said we should
go up over the wall and investigate
but it went straight up and was much
taller than any of the three of us
but Chumley said OK I'll go then just

hoist me up and I'll go right over
so the three of us kind of

crowded together and Chumley stepped
into the ladder we made with our
six arms braced hard by our six legs
and we lifted him up and over

in the stark glare of the afternoon when
no one was watching and he

lifted over much lighter than we thought and
down the other side now totally obscured to us

did Chumley

And then there was just the three of us and no
Chumley because we never saw him again after
that he was gone forever and we

never found out what was going on over there and we

the three of us
never again saw

Chumley

11/2

79 IF ALL THE WOOD IN THE WORLD

If all the wood in the world were to sing

and every rose gave a political speech

and every cloud took pity on its neighbor

and every stone composed an epic poem about
being a stone

and every dust mote were aware of its
mortality as it lay or drifted onto the
curved or flat surfaces of things

and the blind archer let go of his bowstring
and his arrow sang out its target as it
flew through to its intended goal

and the air itself through which it flew
hummed in anticipatory monotones

and water blew wet kisses to the sky

and every flame danced Flamenco
stamping itself out with its own heels until quenched

and each of us saw God direct with our
own eyes in naked vision
as clearly as we see ourselves stooping to
drink from a lake

cupping the water with our hands and
catching our eyes looking back at us
as snowy mountains go up around us to the
peak of the sky

And each of us knows we see this and
acts upon it

and phones ring with the news

But there is no news

It's as old as God
though there be no time with God

and everything is therefore inside-out to
what it seems

and that raw inner surface is
where our existence lies

singing to the clouds and roses
and the blur of things as well as their clarity

and everything stops though it
never stops but only

flows or floats or seems to stop and start so
fast it's like movement but is immobile

as only God moves

though He be motionless

                                                          11/5

80 SWIMMING ON

The fish is happiest when it
doesn't know it's happy

surrounded on all sides by its favorite
element

So the house with peaked roof that just
collapsed under million weight of
snow wasn't at all happy

or the gnats twirling around the light bulb
exchanging jokes and light perceptions
not each of whom can be caught by the
flying hand or swatter though their

season be drawing to a close and they
don't feel as well as they did at
Summer's dawn

As I am happy now with you my
invisible companion giving me words to
compose with almost as fast as my

pen can race along gnat-like and
happy with merely circulating

Water their natural element those

fish in the first stanza blinklessly

swimming on

> 11/7

81 IMPOSSIBLE TO SLEEP

Impossible to sleep
in the antlers of this giant moose

Impossible to sleep
between one screech and the next of a
train wreck that hasn't yet taken place

Impossible to sleep when every tenement inhabitant
opens his or her mouth and sees flames

Impossible to sleep
as cirrus clouds transform ever so slowly into
actual suspended cities about to dissolve forever

Impossible while perfectly sincere imbeciles dictate
what intelligent people in crêpe paper chains should think

Impossible while medicine administered
bloats you like a gas balloon and you
rise and float over your furniture like a proclamation

While government schools use the backs of immigrants as
blackboards and for chalk cutout portions
of their own Constitutions

Impossible to sleep actually while my impending
rheumatism seems to be acting up like an
antenna for sorrows while a goodly

percentage of New Yorkers seems asleep
or at least the irregularly snoring horizon seems to
indicate as much

Though Eskimo babies are wide-eyed wondering if they'll
melt down to Seattle after all

And whales are wondering as they hear the
whaling boats above them whatever happened to
their emergency protection treaties on the high seas

And extraterrestrials are wide-eyed with all their
trillion eyes on the ends of sensitive stalks
wondering whatever happened to the earth they so
loved to look at gathering a fuzz of

emissions gases and hypocrisy around itself

like garishly extravagant furs around a
tyrant's wife stepping on top of the
heads of her subjects to enter her

fresh bone palace

and whose true heartbeat grows fainter in the
milky splash of stars across space the

shape of a knucklebone tapping repeatedly on the

secret door of God

11/10 (New York)

82 KIND OF PERSON

I'm not the kind of person who gets his shoes shined
but go to the plastic box at the bottom of my closet
with the waxes and brushes to do it myself

But I'm also not the kind of person who
works outside all day in the sun getting leathery and
prematurely brown with ox-drawn plows or more
intricate machinery

Nor either he who in brushed cotton and gold tie sits behind a
desk in windowed or windowless cubicles
shifting and prioritizing sheaves of papers

Nor yet he who wanders totally free of well just about
everything through our streets or back alleys leaning down for
bent cigarette butts or scraps

And yet neither in light cotton ministering in
Africa or Asia for the downtrodden with
books and medicines wan smiles and malaria

In fact I'm not so many kinds of persons
similar I imagine to so many
others who are also not so many kinds of
persons in full length or handheld mirrors

or no mirrors but the sky itself on a
clear or cloudy day

upright or supine on this rolling earth
somewhere in a convergence and confluence of

stars and other mighty influences

A palpitation in the void

An anthology of godly and ungodly characteristics
forever tipping the balance one way or the other

wishing for the Clear Entrance and the
Perfect Satisfaction

Hoping for the Best Outcome in a bewilderment of
Options

leaving behind everything at last
to go one step forward as the very person we are

in darkness or light

for all eternity

11/10 (Penn Station)

83   HELD IN THRALL

If mortal pain is a bridge across the
Rubicon of stagnant rejection

uh-huh

If physical pain is a peacock garden of
arrogant tail displays and low-branch screams
enough to awaken the whole zoo

If the pain of our existence is an up-ladder from
the hole we've dug by our insistent personhood
and only by that pain can we overcome it
ironically enough though it may be

and death is simply the black homburg and
spats we need to finish out the routine
along with perhaps a cane and one
stuffed prop of our choice

And the steps leading down are the same as the
steps leading up if we only knew

And if the stage cleared of scenery is also
just another scene to clear away even with its
brick back wall and EXIT door sign glimmering

And if the song we sing in pain either as
gallows humor or actual shouts of
joy out of the flames is true and well-meant

And if all the memories reeling back in
billion millimeter 3-D are
more than a sad commentary on a
short but eventful life still unreeling itself

And if the ship that takes us away to the
island is the same ship that
brought us to the island in the first place with its
sagging rigging and Jolly Roger flapping

And God is One in all these circumstances
in a level field that stretches away as
far as the eye can see and farther

And pain is a little door stood up on it
through which we go on hands and knees and
talking or mumbling our way out of this
from which there is no safe egress

And there's no conclusion for all these
dependent clauses (if that's what they are)

No nice neat denouement to all these
urgencies except He Who is their Origin and
Impetus in the dead of night and in our
excruciating pain remains One in all our
furious multiplications

Then grateful silence may be the great and
gorgeous gazelle-eyes that look back at us
and in whose depthless black irises and
pupils we see the radiant city alit with true
otherworldly light

and wheeling birds and choirs and jubilant sounds so
fine only a needle hair in space can
detect them and broadcast their
chords to the ears of the blind and the
fiery visions of the deaf

in whose pain I'm now so
held in thrall

11/11

84 WAKING

   When the drift of thoughts grows wider

   it's time to sleep

   Waking however

   is another matter

                                    11/12

85 IN THE REALM OF NEITHER

There was a house and the seven architects
who built it

There was Sam and Leonard and Sizak and
Dorothy along with

JD and "the Eel Seller of Samarkand" and Joe

and they all convened in the place where the
house was projected to be though nothing

as yet showed anything but its location

They brought in a diviner to divine how
right or wrong the initial choice was

as well as rid the soil of djinn or demons
and purify the place always a

noble consideration

The seven architects worked day and night they
worked together and apart in teams or in
competition

meeting on Thursday nights around a septagonal table
to present their consensus or lack of consensus and their projects

One envisioned a hill with a cut crystal installation
like a diamond set in its beryl

Another saw wood beams set vertically as if a
forest were just now getting the idea of

a home and slowly growing closer together to
form walls

A third I think Sizak saw various levels with
connecting waterfalls just like his idyllic homeland

Dorothy saw a house suspended somewhat
above the plot and even turning 360 degrees very

gradually by a system of hydraulics
buried underground

The final three were in perfect unity and
under the umbrella of the Eel Seller of Samarkand

kept their plans secret until some of the
elements of the final choice were more apparent

or even under construction

2

God builds the universe in the same way
say the theologians

in that He calls various elements into play which He's given
divine intelligence and molecular movement
that interact and project their vision which is
His vision through their eyes

and plans are drawn up in meticulous detail actually in
His case down to the subatomic structure as well

fashioned by an elegant consensus which in
His case also is His consensus among Himself

and there's even a secret threesome who'll
come into dynamic play once the

subtle structures are committed

and then phenomena rise out of the numina and a
ghostly third appears as
they say those three being
opposites that attract and repel as well as their
peaceful resolution

O rills and rolling brooks O sumptuousness and barrenness aloft and deep within us at

every turn as whirling energies continue the
discontinuous spiral both up and down
outside and within itself

against the backdrop of stars equally involved and
equally fashioned

until houses manifest to house His spiral in
multivalences and intercommunicating intelligences more

various and conscious than we could
ever be aware of from rainforest eyes along a

razor thin leaf to molecular tundra drowsers whispering into
frozen ears deep in the permafrost

3

Then the day comes when a willowy and almost
ectoplasmic structure takes place

If you squint you can almost see it and
imagine inhabiting it

And the Eel Seller knows now his time has
come the mystery may be unfolded and the

supernatural light of his particular intellect
shone on the proceedings

though light is invisible within light just as
darkness is invisible within darkness

and matter is invisible within spirit just as
spirit is invisible within matter

So although a shivering and even an
occasional rumbling takes place and

fingers seem to be flying and sparkling
energies converging

nothing beyond the foremost partitions
could be seen

and the three of them JD the Eel Seller of
Samarkand and Joe sat in their

usual places with their usual inscrutable
expressions on nearly invisible faces

and little by little a breathing takes place just a
kind of groaning and deep-throated

whining as if reluctant to leave its point its womb of
primordial immateriality and then

a rhythmic sighing can be heard and
finally the in and out breathing of a

live entity that is taking shape before us

4

But the inhabitant makes the habitation and
spirit dictates body each time so that

a gnat alone in a small room acts as only a
gnat can trying to find its way out whatever the

Way of the gnat might be so we have a
situation here where God's living intentions are
made manifest in the structures that arise

and winds blow across them both good or
ill as He pleases but the facets that record and

catch those winds are our specifically envisioned
in-dwellings with doors and windows
gabled and cantilevered roofs and

terraces porches and balconies overlooking the
abyss as well as the entire
rest of the cosmos

And looking back at us are identical
structures identically arrived at

out of what is and is not
from the Realm of Neither in which He does and does not

reside and all else resides comfortably or

uncomfortably as He sees fit from His
involved and uninvolved perspective each

crystalline sliver or hinge in perfect place by His

comprehensively
mutual agreement

alone

11/12

ABOUT THE AUTHOR

Born in 1940 in Oakland, California, Daniel Abdal-Hayy Moore's first book of poems, *Dawn Visions*, was published by Lawrence Ferlinghetti of City Lights Books, San Francisco, in 1964, and the second in 1972, *Burnt Heart/Ode to the War Dead*. He created and directed *The Floating Lotus Magic Opera Company* in Berkeley, California in the late 60s, and presented two major productions, *The Walls Are Running Blood*, and *Bliss Apocalypse*. He became a Sufi Muslim in 1970, performed the Hajj in 1972, and lived and traveled throughout Morocco, Spain, Algeria and Nigeria, landing in California and publishing *The Desert is the Only Way Out*, and *Chronicles of Akhira* in the early 80s (Zilzal Press). Residing in Philadelphia since 1990, in 1996 he published *The Ramadan Sonnets* (Jusoor/City Lights), and in 2002, *The Blind Beekeeper* (Jusoor/Syracuse University Press). He has been the major editor for a number of works, including *The Burdah* of Shaykh Busiri, translated by Shaykh Hamza Yusuf, and the poetry of Palestinian poet, Mahmoud Darwish, translated by Munir Akash. He is also widely published on the worldwide web: *The American Muslim, DeenPort*, and his own website and poetry blog, among others: www.danielmoorepoetry.com, www.ecstaticxchange.wordpress.com. He is also currently poetry editor for *Seasons Journal* and *Islamica Magazine*. The Ecstatic Exchange Series is bringing out the extensive body of his works of poetry (a complete list of published works on page 2).

POETIC WORKS BY DANIEL ABDAL-HAYY MOORE
Published and Unpublished

Dawn Visions (published by City Lights, 1964)
Burnt Heart/Ode to the War Dead (published by City Lights, 1972)
This Body of Black Light Gone Through the Diamond (printed by Fred Stone,
    Cambridge, Mass, 1965)
On The Streets at Night Alone (1965?)
All Hail the Surgical Lamp (1967)
States of Amazement (1970)

Abdallah Jones and the Disappearing-Dust Caper (published by The Ecstatic Exchange/
    Crescent Series, 2006)
The Chronicles of Akhira (1981) (published by Zilzal Press with Typoglyphs by Karl
    Kempton, 1986)
Mouloud (1984) (A Zilzal Press chapbook, 1995)
Man is the Crown of Creation (1984)
The Look of the Lion (The Parabolas of Sight) (1984)
The Desert is the Only Way Out (completed 4/21/84) (Zilzal Press chapbook, 1985)
Atomic Dance (1984) (am here books, 1988)
Outlandish Tales (1984)
Awake as Never Before (12/26/84) (Zilzal Press chapbook, 1993)
Glorious Intervals (1/1/85) (Zilzal Press chapbook, ?)
Long Days on Earth/Book I (1/28 – 8/30/85)
Long Days on Earth/Book II (Hayy Ibn Yaqzan)
Long Days on Earth/Book III (1/22/86)
Long Days on Earth/Book IV (1986)
The Ramadan Sonnets (Long Days on Earth/Book V) (5/9 – 6/11/86) (Published by
    Jusoor/City Lights Books, 1996) (Republished as **Ramadan Sonnets** by
    The Ecstatic Exchange, 2005)
Long Days on Earth/Book VI (6-8/30/86)
Holograms (9/4/86 – 3/26/87)
History of the World (The Epic of Man's Survival) (4/7 – 6/18/87)
Exploratory Odes (6/25 – 10/18/87)
The Man at the End of the World (11/11 – 12/10/87)
The Perfect Orchestra (3/30 – 7/25/88)
Fed from Underground Springs (7/30 – 11/23/88)
Ideas of the Heart (11/27/88 – 5/5/89)
New Poems (scattered poems, out of series, from 3/24 – 8/9/89)
Facing Mecca (5/16 – 11/11/89)
A Maddening Disregard for the Passage of Time (11/17/89 – 5/20/90)
The Heart Falls in Love with Visions of Perfection (6/15/90 – 6/2/91)

Like When You Wave at a Train and the Train Hoots Back at You (Farid's Book)
 (6/11 – 7/26/91) (Published by The Ecstatic Exchange, 2008)
Orpheus Meets Morpheus (8/1/91– 3/14/92)
The Puzzle (3/21/92 – 8/17/93)
The Greater Vehicle (10/17/93 – 4/30/94)
A Hundred Little 3-D Pictures (5/14/94 – 9/11/95)
The Angel Broadcast (9/29 – 12/17/95)
Mecca/Medina Time-Warp (12/19/95 – 1/6/96) (Published as a Zilzal Press chapbook, 1996)
Miracle Songs for the Millennium (1/20 – 10/16/96)
The Blind Beekeeper (11/15/96 – 5/30/97) (Published 2002 by Jusoor/Syracuse University Press)
Chants for the Beauty Feast (6/3 – 10/28/97)
Open Doors (10/29/97 – 5/23/98)
Salt Prayers (5/29 – 10/24/98) (Published by The Ecstatic Exchange, 2005)
Some (10/25/98 – 4/25/99)
Flight to Egypt (5/1 – 5/16/99)
I Imagine a Lion (5/21 – 11/15/99)(Published by The Ecstatic Exchange, 2006)
Millennial Prognostications (11/25/99 – 2/2/2000)
The Book of Infinite Beauty (2/4 – 10/8/2000)
Blood Songs (10/9/2000 – 4/3/2001)
The Music Space (4/10 – 9/16/2001) (Published by The Ecstatic Exchange, 2007)
Where Death Goes (9/20/2001 – 5/1/2002)
The Flame of Transformation Turns to Light (99 Ghazals Written in English) (5/14 – 8/21/2002) (Published by The Ecstatic Exchange, 2007)
Through Rose-Colored Glasses (7/22/2002 – 1/15/2003) (Published by The Ecstatic Exchange, 2008)
Psalms for the Broken-Hearted (1/22 – 5/25/2003) (Published by The Ecstatic Exchange, 2006)
Hoopoe's Argument (5/27 – 9/18/03)
Love is a Letter Burning in a High Wind (9/21 – 11/6/2003) (Published by The Ecstatic Exchange, 2006)
Laughing Buddha/Weeping Sufi (11/7/2003 – 1/10/2004) (Published by The Ecstatic Exchange, 2005)
Mars and Beyond (1/20 – 3/29/2004) (Published by The Ecstatic Exchange, 2005)
Underwater Galaxies (4/5 – 7/21/2004) (Published by The Ecstatic Exchange, 2007)
Cooked Oranges (7/23/2004 – 1/24/2005 (Published by The Ecstatic Exchange, 2007)
Holiday from the Perfect Crime (1/25 – 6/11/2005)
Stories Too Fiery to Sing Too Watery to Whisper (6/13 – 10/24/2005)
Coattails of the Saint (10/26/2005 – 5/10/2006) (Published by The Ecstatic Exchange, 2006)
In the Realm of Neither (5/14/2006 – 11/12/06) (Published by The Ecstatic Exchange, 2008)
Invention of the Wheel (11/13/06 – 6/10/07)
The Sound of Geese Over the House (6/15 – 11/4/07)

The Fire Eater's Lunchbreak (11/10/07 – 5/19/08)
Sparks Off the Main Strike (5/23/08 –)

www.ingramcontent.com/pod-product-compliance
Lightning Source LLC
Chambersburg PA
CBHW020854090426
42736CB00008B/373